LOCOMOTION

To my Dad, thank you for everything – especially the love of railways! – A.S.

BIG PICTURE PRESS

First published in the UK in 2022 by Big Picture Press,
an imprint of Bonnier Books UK,
4th Floor, Victoria House,
Bloomsbury Square, London, WC1B 4DA
Owned by Bonnier Books
Sveavägen 56, Stockholm, Sweden
www.bonnierbooks.co.uk

1 3 5 7 9 10 8 6 4 2

ISBN 978-1-78741-750-2

This book was typeset in Modern Appliances, Founders Grotesk and Avenir.
The illustrations were created and coloured digitally.

Edited by Joanna McInerney
Designed by Olivia Cook
Production by Ché Creasey

Printed in China

ALASTAIR STEELE

RYO TAKEMASA

LOCOMOTION

CONTENTS

INTRODUCTION. 6

THE FIRST RAILWAYS 8

STEAM LOCOMOTIVES. 10

RAILWAYS OF THE WORLD: THE FFESTINIOG RAILWAY 12

ELECTRIC LOCOMOTIVES 14

DIESEL LOCOMOTIVES. 15

PASSENGER TRAINS 16

RAILWAYS OF THE WORLD: THE ORIENT EXPRESS. 18

FREIGHT TRAINS 20

RAILWAYS OF THE WORLD: THE BAIKONUR COSMODROME 22

MAIL BY RAIL. 24

MAKING CONNECTIONS 26

OVERCOMING OBSTACLES. 28

RAILWAYS OF THE WORLD: THE CALIFORNIA ZEPHYR. 30

MOUNTAIN RAILWAYS 32

RAILWAYS OF THE WORLD: THE DARJEELING HIMALAYAN RAILWAY. . . . 34

STATIONS 36

MASS RAPID TRANSIT. 38

TRAMS 40

SKY LINES 42

COMPLETE CONTROL. 44

RAILWAYS AT WAR. 46

RAILWAYS OF THE WORLD: THE PRINCESS CHRISTIAN 48

END OF THE GOLDEN AGE. 50

HIGH-SPEED RAIL. 52

RAILWAYS OF THE WORLD: THE SHINKANSEN 54

INTO THE FUTURE 56

TRAIN TIMELINE 58

RECORD BREAKERS AROUND THE WORLD 60

GLOSSARY 62

INDEX 64

INTRODUCTION

From the moment humans first began to explore the world, it became a priority to be able to move ever further and faster. We walked, swam and ran, invented the wheel and learned how to domesticate animals, all to aid the progress of human life. Today, we can travel any way we want to; we can ride, drive or fly – we can even explore space. Food can be shipped around the world, mail can be sent by air and messages over the Internet.

But wind the clock back a few hundred years and the story looked rather different. Before the Industrial Revolution of the 18th century, options for travel were severely limited, and in nearly all cases travelling by horseback was the only way to get around if you didn't want to walk. Slow, uncomfortable and offering little protection from the weather, it was still the most effective way to travel as luxurious horse-drawn carriages were expensive.

The other option was water transport. Sea travel could help to move larger loads across greater distances, but sailing ships were heavily dependent on wind patterns, and changes in weather could make these voyages dangerous. In addition to the perils of the journey by sea, it was also time-consuming. A trip to India from England by ship could take up to six months, for example.

Inland rivers were also navigable by boats, and became an important way to transport goods. Many cities, such as London, Rome and Cairo, were built around them. When the Industrial Revolution began to take off, human-made canals expanded the river system, and became important to the booming economy. Horse-drawn canal boats were able to pull a boat a hundred times their own weight on land, and this made moving heavy goods easier. However, the pace was still slow, and even bigger loads couldn't meet the insatiable demands of the revolution. Another solution was needed...

Enter, the age of the railway!

THE FIRST RAILWAYS

Today, railways are commonplace in many parts of the world. They snake around our coastlines, zip across our countryside and transport goods and millions of passengers every single day. It is strange to think that they have only been around as we know them for about two hundred years.

Railways existed long before the first steam engines were invented. These 'railways' appeared in Europe during the 17th century and were designed to make manual work easier. Heavy loads were moved via four-wheeled wagons, which ran on wooden planks. The reduced **friction** made moving materials like stone and coal much quicker and easier.

The first steam engines were used in British mines during the 17th century to pump water. It wasn't long before engineers tried using steam power to propel vehicles, and in 1802 the inventor Richard Trevithick built the very first working steam locomotive.

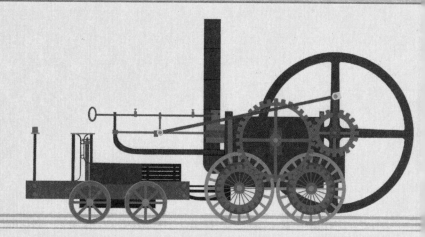

Once the idea of steam locomotives caught on, there was no looking back. *Puffing Billy,* built by William Hedley (a leading industrial engineer of the 19th century) in 1813, is the oldest surviving locomotive in the world. Hedley pioneered the use of smooth metal rails, which provided lower friction than wooden rails, making it possible to haul even heavier loads.

Puffing Billy went on to influence many other engineers. The first public railway to use steam locomotives, the Stockton and Darlington Railway in England, opened in 1825. It was designed by George Stephenson, who went on to be known as the 'Father of Railways' for his influential role in so many early schemes.

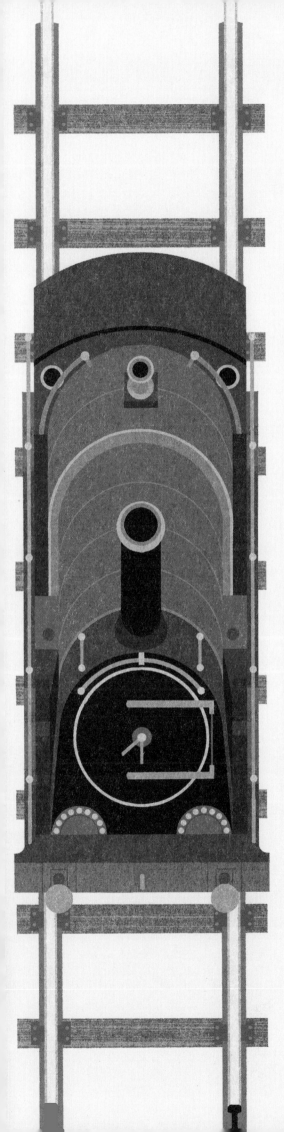

THE GAUGE

One of Stephenson's most significant decisions was to set the gauge for British railways. The gauge is the distance between the rails and is measured from the inside edge of one rail to the other. By using the same gauge on different railways, Stephenson could ensure that the lines were compatible when they connected. He decided on a gauge of 1,435mm, which became known as the 'standard gauge'. Today, more than half of the world's railways use this gauge.

The standard gauge was not without its rivals. Isambard Kingdom Brunel, engineer of the British Great Western Railway, decided on a much wider gauge when he designed the line between London and Bristol, which opened in 1838. His wider tracks, set at a width of 2,144mm, allowed for more stability at speed, and bigger vehicles which could carry greater loads. Unfortunately for Brunel, his ideas arrived too late to compete, and by 1892 all the tracks had been converted to the narrower gauge of his rival, Stephenson.

STEAM LOCOMOTIVES

Once the possibility of steam-powered engines had been realised, a whole host of locomotives were tried and tested around the world. Some proved too heavy, others too unreliable and some were even dangerous, but the arrival of one revolutionary design changed the course of history. *Rocket*, designed by engineer Robert Stephenson (George Stephenson's son – see page 8) was to provide the principles of design for the vast majority of steam locomotives that followed.

Steam **locomotives** need water and fuel to run. The fuel (usually coal) is burnt in a fire at one end of the boiler in an area known as the **firebox**. To fan the flames, air is channelled in from below to provide the oxygen needed for the fire to burn intensely.

Heat from the fire passes through the **boiler** via smaller tubes. This heats the water to boiling point, raising the steam pressure.

As the pressure builds, the steam is directed to the **cylinders**. These are controlled by valves, which act like a gearbox in a car. The steam presses down on a **piston** inside the cylinders, moving the wheels via a rod which connects them.

ROCKET

A crucial part of *Rocket's* revolutionary design was its boiler. Multiple tubes ran through it from the fire, which enlarged the surface area and heated the water more easily. A blast pipe was used to send steam from the cylinders into the chimney, helping to pull the hot gases along the tubes. More steam meant more power and increased efficiency. Boilers using tubes and blast pipes like *Rocket* became the standard from this point onwards.

THE FFESTINIOG RAILWAY

The Ffestiniog railway in North Wales is a marvel of 19th century engineering. It was built to transport slate for roof tiles from the quarries around the town of Blaenau Ffestiniog, high up in the mountains of Snowdonia, down to the harbour at Porthmadog. It opened in 1836, using a narrow gauge of 597mm to match the wagons already in use in the quarries.

The original trains were powered by horses, which hauled empty wagons uphill. The designer of the railway, James Spooner, made sure the route was downhill all the way from the quarries, so the loaded wagons could roll down to the harbour. The trains were controlled by brakesmen – groups of two or three men who rode on the loaded wagons to control the trains' speed. Only some of the wagons had brakes, which were applied by pulling a lever. With some trains up to one hundred wagons long, the brakesmen had to jump between the moving wagons to apply or release the brakes, which was incredibly dangerous.

By the 1860s, the railway was generating so much work carrying slate that the horses couldn't keep up. There was also increasing demand for a passenger service, which meant the railway had to be reworked. The solution was for several small steam engines to be built, which were among the first narrow gauge locomotives in the world. By 1869, there were six working the line, but soon even they began to struggle with the demand.

Luckily, a revolutionary idea was presented to the railway that same year. Engineer Robert Francis Fairlie had patented the 'Double Fairlie', an ingenious double-ended locomotive design. This was in effect two locomotives constructed back-to-back and running on a pair of **bogies**, which saved the expense of having two crews but doubled the power output. The first of these was called *Little Wonder*, and over the next 17 years another three Double Fairlie's were built for the railway. They were so successful that Robert Fairlie allowed the railway to use his **patent** for free forever, something it continues to do to this day.

ELECTRIC LOCOMOTIVES

The first electric train was tested as far back as 1837. Unlike steam
trains, electric locomotives do not carry fuel on-board. Instead, they
are powered by electricity which can be supplied from overhead lines,
a third rail or in storage such as batteries. Because electric trains can
be powered by renewable energy sources, they are considered less
polluting than steam or diesel trains.

The first electric passenger train was presented by Werner von Siemens at an exhibition in Berlin in 1879.
Consisting of a small locomotive and three cars, it reached a speed of just 13km/h.

The *ETR 200* is a record-breaking electric passenger train. It is widely considered one of the first ever high-speed
trains and was put into service in 1936. In 1939, it broke the speed record for trains by reaching just over 201km/h.

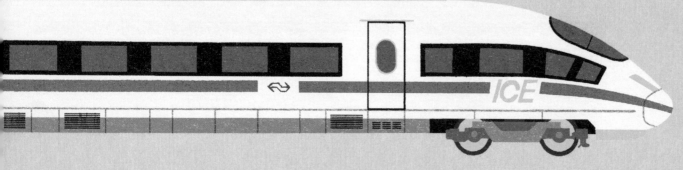

The *ICE* (Intercity Express) is one of Germany's most successful electric trains. The third generation *ICE 3*,
can reach speeds of 300km/h. Since 2018, it has run on entirely **renewable energy** sources.

DIESEL LOCOMOTIVES

In a diesel locomotive, the power comes from an engine that burns diesel oil. While a steam locomotive needed two people to crew it and hours to attain the right steam pressure, a diesel locomotive could simply be switched on and driven away, making them much easier and much cheaper to run. Rudolf Diesel patented his first diesel engine in 1898, but it wasn't until around 1912 that they were first used in a locomotive.

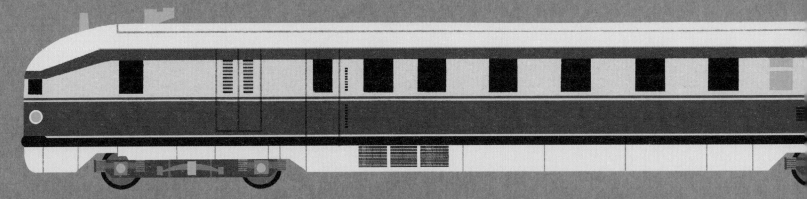

The famous *DRG Class SVT 877 Hamburg Flyer,* often referred to as the 'Flying Hamburger', was first put into service in 1933. Its smooth, rounded shape was influenced by Zeppelin **airships** allowing for minimal air resistance.

The *Deltic*, built in 1956, was considered the most powerful diesel locomotive in the world at that time.

The *Intercity 125* is one of the most successful diesel trains of all time. So named because it was designed to cruise at 125 mph (about 201km/h) when in service, it also holds the all-time speed record for diesel trains of 238km/h, which it reached in 1987.

PASSENGER TRAINS

Railways changed the way people travelled forever. They provided what may have been the first opportunities for people to travel far from their home, to experience new sights and to consider new ways of working. Today, they play a vital role in transporting people for business or pleasure.

The Swansea and Mumbles Railway in the UK was the first passenger-carrying railway, opening in 1807 along its horse-drawn route. By 1830, passenger-carrying steam trains appeared on the Liverpool and Manchester Railway, and trains soon evolved rapidly. Carriages grew in length and splendour, gaining extra wheels to provide smoother journeys. Interiors became more comfortable, from the inclusion of padded seats, to toilets and restaurants. But not everyone enjoyed these benefits straight away. It wasn't until 1844 that the UK passed the Railway Regulation Act. Before then, some passengers often travelled in cramped open-air wagons, without seats and on limited services.

EXPRESS TRAINS

Once railways became more established, passenger trains began to run more frequently and became more affordable. The development of the railways, alongside the booming steamship industry, allowed for widespread **migration**, particularly from Europe into North America, as people went in search of new job opportunities and places to live.

Today, a variety of service types are on offer. Local trains, made up of only a few carriages, call at every station and take a long time to cover a route. Others might stop at fewer stations but have more carriages and travel a bit quicker – these are often called 'semi-fast' trains. The fastest of all, and usually the most glamorous, are express trains. Express trains only stop at main stations or might even run non-stop between two cities. The famous *Flying Scotsman* (shown above), which ran from London to Edinburgh in the UK, or the *Empire State Express* in the US, represent the Golden Age of the express train.

THE ORIENT EXPRESS

There are few more evocative names than the *Orient Express*. Made famous by its luxurious passenger experience and picturesque route through romantic cities such as Paris, Vienna and Budapest, its beauty has been immortalised in both film and literature.

The train was the idea of Georges Nagelmackers, the founder of the Compagnie Internationale des Wagons-Lits, which specialised in high-class, long-distance railway travel. The *Orient Express* was the jewel in its crown offering a grand service in both its dining and sleeping cars, for a trip that covered nearly 3,200km, and lasted 67 hours. Passengers were greeted by polished marbled bathrooms, velvet drapery, oriental rugs and soft leather armchairs. At its height, the *Orient Express* carriages were

painted in a beautiful deep blue **livery**, with gold detailing. Every carriage had a conductor dressed in a smart uniform, which included a number on the collar that passengers could refer to if they had a complaint to make!

Changing fashions and new travel options such as air and high-speed rail meant that the last descendant of Georges Nagelmackers' train ran in 2009, but its spirit and name lives on. Today, the modern *Orient Express* serves a route from London to Venice via Paris and uses beautifully restored vintage carriages to give travellers an unequalled level of luxury. While being serenaded by the on-board pianist, passengers are treated to feasts such as lobster, caviar and peach melba.

FREIGHT TRAINS

Some of the longest, heaviest and most powerful trains in the world are freight trains, which help to move heavy or bulky goods. The earliest freight trains sprang from a need to move raw materials such as coal or metal ores to industrial centres, and today they not only continue to move raw materials but distribute finished products too. The distances covered can be huge – even intercontinental – with some services running all the way from China to Europe.

Freight trains are usually formed of a locomotive and many separate wagons. These locomotives are not designed for speed, but power. Whether diesel or electric, one train with one driver is a far more efficient way of hauling goods over a long distance than travelling by road and using lots of lorries.

Early freight trains used small, basic wagons to transport goods. The brakes were often only installed on the locomotive and at the rear end of the train, so the goods had to be driven slowly and carefully. Modern wagons have their own brakes, controlled by the driver. All manner of products are transported by freight train – milk tankers, stone hoppers, mineral wagons and even **transporter wagons** carrying road vehicles. Freight can also be loaded into shipping containers, making it easy to transport goods to ships for onward travel.

THE BAIKONUR COSMODROME

Sometimes, freight can take unusual forms. The Baikonur Cosmodrome in Kazakhstan is one of the few places on Earth where spacecraft are launched. In fact, nowhere else in the world launches as many spacecraft as this site does.

The railway system at Baikonur is the largest industrial network in the world and is designed to transport entire spacecraft from the assembly building to the launch pad, ready for their journey into space. It is incredible to think that rockets are constructed and transported via railways at this desert location here on Earth. It is where both *Sputnik*, the first ever satellite, was launched in 1957, and where Yuri Gagarin, the first person in space, was launched in 1961.

In order to transport these enormous **cargoes**, a special type of freight vehicle called a Schnabel car is required. Schnabel cars are designed for oversized cargoes and can withstand huge amounts of weight. They are constructed in two halves which separate to accept the load, similarly to a bird's beak opening and closing. Once secured, the freight is integrated as part of the car itself.

While Schnabel cars can carry rockets, at Baikonur there have been times when even larger loads have been transported. In the 1980s, the Soviet Union developed a space shuttle named *Buran,* which was so large it was pulled to the launch pad by four diesel locomotives on a special railway made from two sets of parallel rails.

MAIL BY RAIL

Freight doesn't always have to be big. Sometimes, even the lightest of goods need an efficient way of being transported. To move mail by rail, several extraordinary ideas allowed for post to be collected and delivered without trains even having to stop. At one time, the mail industry in the UK accounted for over a billion tonnes of letters, postcards, stamps, parcels and boxes a year.

In 1838, the world's first Travelling Post Office (known as the TPO) came into use in the UK. This type of railway carriage enabled staff to sort post en route and was used for over 160 years. TPOs were equipped with 'pigeon-holes' on-board where letters were sorted, and some trains even had a letterbox built in the side of it so people could post letters while it was at a station.

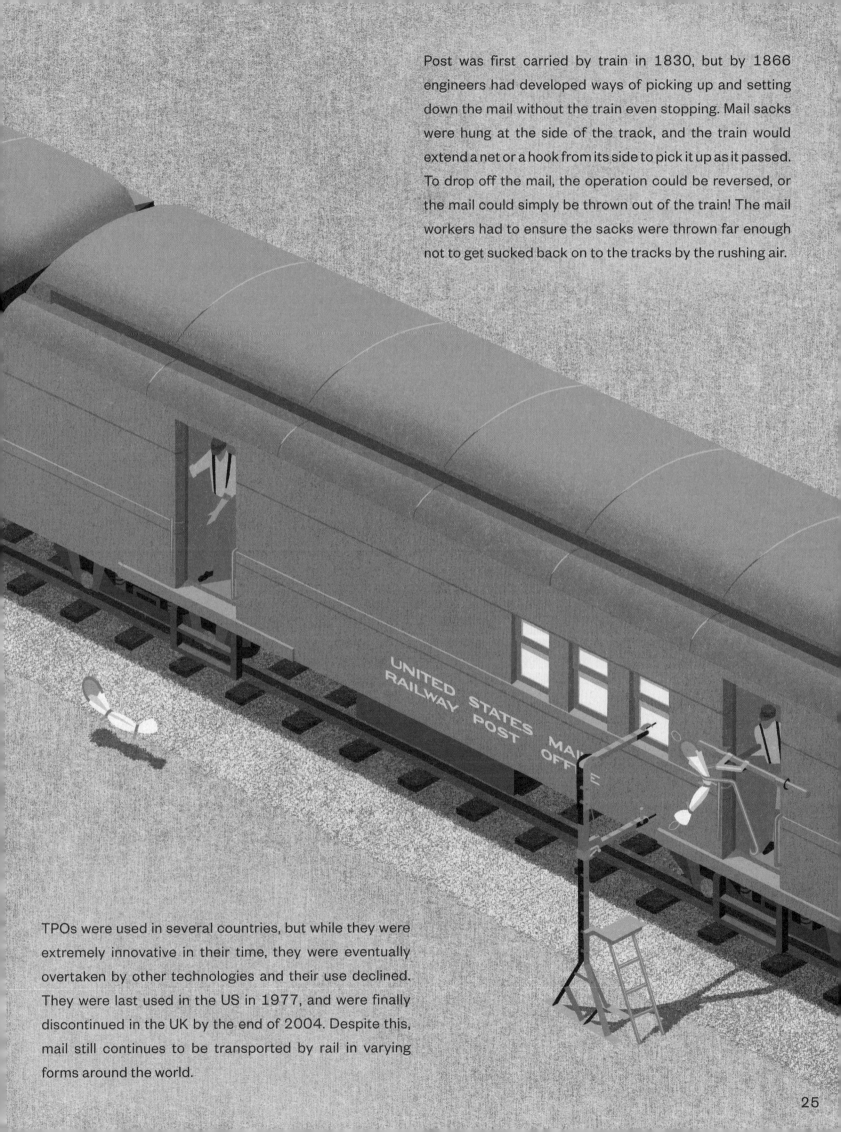

Post was first carried by train in 1830, but by 1866 engineers had developed ways of picking up and setting down the mail without the train even stopping. Mail sacks were hung at the side of the track, and the train would extend a net or a hook from its side to pick it up as it passed. To drop off the mail, the operation could be reversed, or the mail could simply be thrown out of the train! The mail workers had to ensure the sacks were thrown far enough not to get sucked back on to the tracks by the rushing air.

TPOs were used in several countries, but while they were extremely innovative in their time, they were eventually overtaken by other technologies and their use declined. They were last used in the US in 1977, and were finally discontinued in the UK by the end of 2004. Despite this, mail still continues to be transported by rail in varying forms around the world.

MAKING CONNECTIONS

As technology became more advanced at the start of the 1800s, the world began to feel smaller. The opening of the first intercity railway between Liverpool and Manchester in the UK meant passengers and goods could be moved at record speeds. New railways began to spring up all over the world. But travelling across longer distances presented new problems too.

MAP
OF
THE GREAT
TRANS-SIBERIAN ROUTE

MOSCOW

Today, we think very little of international time zones, but before railways were introduced, time was measured by the position of the sun and was therefore much more localised. So how were trains able to run to one timetable between two distant cities? The answer was to standardise time, so every clock across the country displayed the same thing. This transition occurred in the UK during 1847, when all railways adopted what became known as Greenwich Mean Time.

Arrived in the heart of Siberia around breakfast time. It is bitterly cold and there is a strong wind blowing. The landscape looks extraordinarily wild – flat country with little glistening lakes here and there, which look beautiful against the sunrise.

It really does seem like we are at the end of the world.

VLADIVOSTOK

While standardising time across a small country may have been relatively easy, doing so across enormous continents, thousands of kilometres wide was another matter. In 1869, the first **transcontinental** railway in the US was completed, connecting the east and west coasts by rail for the first time – an amazing feat that took just six years to finish. The need for more uniformed time-keeping grew, and that same year the first proposals were put forward to divide the country into zones. Today, there are six time zones across the US. With this major obstacle now overcome, transcontinental railways developed rapidly and began to spread.

In Asia, the first transcontinental railway was completed with the opening of the Trans-Siberian Railway in 1916, which runs through Russia. At nearly 10,000km long, it is the longest railway in the world, running from Moscow in the west, to Vladivostok on the shore of the Sea of Japan in the east. It can take a whole week to complete the spectacular journey, which passes through eight time zones, calls at 80 towns and cities, crosses 16 rivers and climbs several mountain ranges.

OVERCOMING OBSTACLES

When railway pioneers first began to build lines across continents, many areas were not well-mapped. Explorers risked their lives to find ways through difficult terrain such as mountain ranges, deserts, canyons and rivers. Their research helped to draw accurate maps, which were used to plan railway routes. Some natural obstacles could be avoided by meandering around them, but for others, ingenious engineering solutions were required to allow trains to pass through. Early bridges were constructed from timber, iron and stone, and were later replaced by steel and concrete, which were quicker and cheaper to use.

The Glenfinnan Viaduct in the Scottish Highlands rose to fame when it was featured in the Harry Potter™ films to showcase the journey of the magical *Hogwarts Express*. Completed in 1898, the concrete **viaduct** features 21 arches.

The Lethbridge Viaduct in Canada is the longest, and highest, **trestle bridge** in the world at 1.6km long, and 96m tall. It was designed as a means of travelling from one side of the prairie to the other without steep gradients.

The Danyang-Kunshan Grand Bridge in China is currently the world's longest bridge, stretching 165km over the Yangtze River. More than 10,000 people were involved in its construction, which took around four years to complete. Incredibly, it is capable of withstanding typhoons and at least magnitude 8 earthquakes.

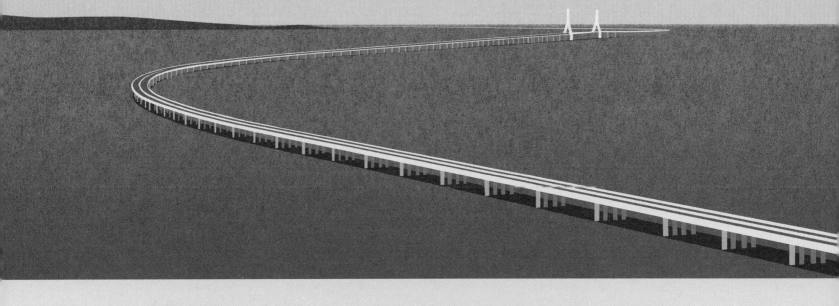

Representing a key milestone in the history of railway engineering, the Forth Bridge in Scotland is a major landmark. Opened in 1890, the Forth Bridge is in fact the longest **cantilever bridge** in the world at 2,467m long.

Opened in 2016 and bored using revolutionary **tunnel boring machines**, (see page 39), the Gotthard Base Tunnel in Switzerland is both the longest railway tunnel and the deepest tunnel used for any traffic in the world. It stretches for almost 60km, with a maximum depth of 2,450m beneath the Alps above it.

THE CALIFORNIA ZEPHYR

The *California Zephyr* is one of the most spectacular long-distance passenger services in the US. Travelling between Chicago and San Francisco, the iconic journey passes through seven states, covering almost 4,000km in just over two days. Following the Colorado River through deep, winding gorges, the train also passes some astonishing scenery along the way, from the snow-capped peaks of the Sierra Nevada mountain range to the alpine forests of the Rocky Mountains.

By crossing such a large swathe of the country, the *California Zephyr* route also includes some of the most incredible feats of American engineering. At the point which it passes through the state border from Illinois into Iowa, the train crosses over the Mississippi River via the Burlington Bridge, a steel girder bridge that

stretches over 650m. It later reaches the Mile High City of Denver (so-called because it is almost exactly one mile (1.6km) above sea level), before climbing the Rocky Mountains, gaining height via the famous 'Big Ten Curve' on its way up.

Because the journey can't be done in a single day, there are some very special types of carriage used in the train. Many have extra windows in the ceilings for passengers to enjoy the mountain views and there are also dining cars for passengers to enjoy hot meals. Most importantly, the train also has sleeping cars. These contain cabins that have beds, which can be stowed away during the day to form seats but fold down to allow for a comfortable night's sleep.

MOUNTAIN RAILWAYS

As trains cannot ascend hills easily, railway lines need to be kept as level as possible. Railways work well because the low amount of friction between wheel and rail means heavy loads can glide along easily. On level track and gentle gradients, this lack of friction is what gives trains their efficiency, but with more severe climbs found on valleys, mountains and hills, the lack of friction becomes problematic. More ingenious engineering solutions are required to tackle these challenges.

One of the simplest ways for a train to ascend a steep incline is to use a rack and pinion system. A toothed pinion wheel is mounted on the axles of the train or locomotive, which mesh with the corresponding teeth of the rack rail, allowing the train to climb up very steep railways with extra grip.

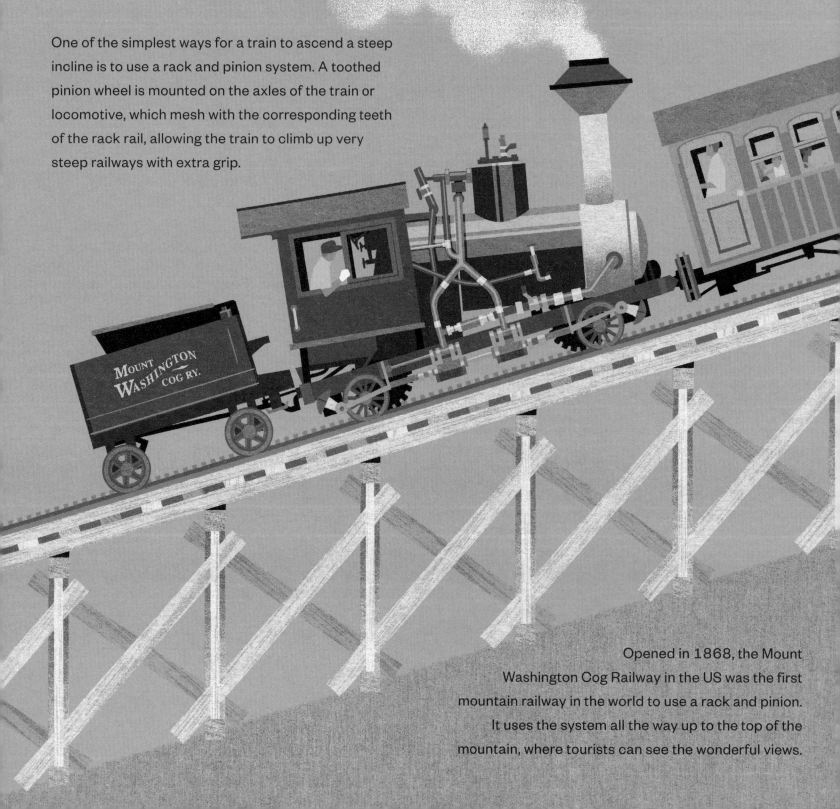

Opened in 1868, the Mount Washington Cog Railway in the US was the first mountain railway in the world to use a rack and pinion. It uses the system all the way up to the top of the mountain, where tourists can see the wonderful views.

FUNICULAR RAILWAYS

Funicular railways are specially designed to move
carriages or trams up and down hills over short distances.
They work via a cable system, which was originally
developed for hoisting freight wagons in quarries, whereby
a heavier descending load is used to pull a lighter load up a
slope. Today, most funiculars are electric passenger lines,
but some older examples use water power. The Schwyz-
Stoos funicular railway in Switzerland is currently the
steepest in the world, climbing over 700m.

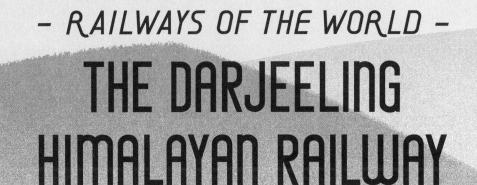

THE DARJEELING HIMALAYAN RAILWAY

The Darjeeling Himalayan Railway, or DHR, is one of the most incredible mountain railways in the world. Its tiny narrow-gauge trains (nicknamed 'toy trains') are so highly valued that the railway is included on UNESCO's list of protected World Heritage Sites.

Opened in 1879 to a gauge of just 610mm, the spectacular line is 88km long and climbs 2,000m over its route, reaching its **summit** at Ghum, the highest railway station in India, at 2.25km above sea level. The railway follows the route of an earlier cart road, which snakes its way up through the extreme landscape, squeezing past tiny towns and trackside markets, and clinging to cliff edges as it passes tea gardens and lush forests.

The DHR doesn't employ any special ways of climbing like a rack and pinion system, yet is still considered one of the most inventive feats of engineering. Because the cart road was in some places too steep for the railway to follow, engineers built in frequent loops and zigzags (known as reverse sidings) where the trains curve their way up the hill to meet the road further on.

Aside from height, the railway also has to cope with the extreme weather of the Himalayas. Monsoon season can bring relentless rain and flooding, and whole sections of the railway are regularly washed away. Such is its value, the track is rebuilt every time, though not always on quite the same route. Over the years, the railway has gained and lost sections of track to cope with the changing landscape after each monsoon, but the trains always find a way of reaching Darjeeling.

STATIONS

From vast mainline and international termini to the smallest unmanned countryside platforms, stations are where railway journeys begin. They have come a long way since the first stations were built, with many stations becoming icons of architecture in their own right.

Maputo station in Mozambique has become a landmark of the city. Completed in 1916, the stunning **façade** features a copper-clad central dome, marble-pillared verandas and wrought-iron latticework. It regularly features as one of the most beautiful railway stations in the world.

Liège-Guillemins in Belgium is a spectacular example of modern design. With a huge curved exterior made of steel, glass and concrete, the station was built to reflect its position at the forefront of technology, as it services the high-speed TGV lines (see page 53) between Paris and Cologne.

Built during the reign of Queen Victoria by British architect Claude Batley, the Chhatrapati Shivaji Maharaj Terminus in Mumbai, India is a stunning example of eastern and western design. Recognised as a UNESCO World Heritage Site, it is the location of the first passenger train service in India. Over three million people pour through its doors every day.

With 44 platforms (more than any other in the world), Grand Central Terminal in New York, US serves the commuter rail lines into the centre of Manhattan. Around 750,000 people pass through the station every day. Because of this, a number of facilities are provided, from food and refreshments to retail opportunities. But that's not all – during its history, Grand Central has included a library, a tennis court and even a cinema.

Of course, station staff are essential to the smooth-running of every journey. From those in the booking office selling tickets, to others on the platform helping to dispatch trains, they all ensure that timekeeping and passenger safety are at the heart of railway operations.

MASS RAPID TRANSIT

Mass Rapid Transit is the term used to describe a transport network which only operates within the limits of a city. They are more familiarly known as subways, metropolitan or underground lines. The success of railways during the 19th century attracted more people and traffic to city centres, causing congestion above ground. New solutions were needed to transport people from place to place quickly and trains yet again held the answer.

Underground railways could bypass congestion above ground and other inconveniences including buildings, parks and rivers. It was therefore possible to transport huge numbers of passengers across town quickly and frequently. Still hugely popular today, rapid transit systems can travel both above and below ground, and have exclusive right-of-way, meaning pedestrians or other vehicles are not permitted to share the track.

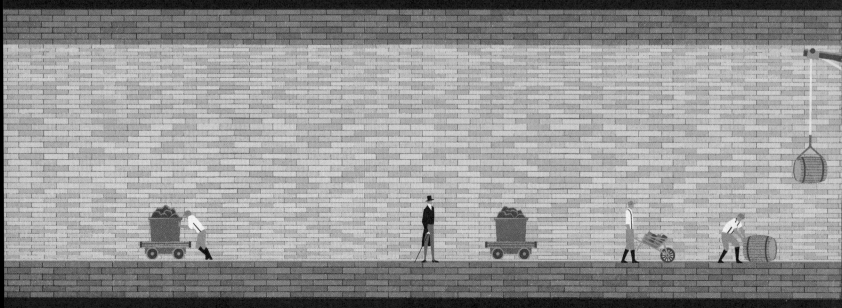

The world's first underground railway opened in London, UK, in 1866, to packed carriages and cheering commuters. It was aptly named the Metropolitan Railway, and transported over 38,000 people on its first day of service. Today, the 'Tube' network (as it is commonly known) transports over two million people every day.

BUILDING THE METROPOLITAN

The Metropolitan Railway was hailed as 'the great engineering triumph of the day', but how was this underground network created? Many of the shallow tunnels were built using a method called 'cut and cover'. This is where the ground is first dug out to make a trench, then covered over to form a tunnel. Later, **'tunnelling shields'** were used (shown left), a revolutionary concept patented by engineer Marc Brunel. The shield allowed for the first successful tunnel underneath a river to be built, and paved the way for the tunnel boring machines of the future (see page 29).

TRAMS

Most railways are built to deliberately avoid other types of vehicle, but tramways are a special type of railway which run on rails laid in public roads. Tramlines are usually built in cities to help transfer people quickly and easily around town and can often be seen criss-crossing major cities like Melbourne or Rome. Before the widespread use of buses or taxis, trams were an extremely popular form of transport.

Early trams were horse-drawn, but later urban tramways were among the first types of railway to make widespread use of electric power. Most electric trams work via a power cable (known as an overhead line) that is suspended above the tramlines along the entire route. Each tramcar has a **pantograph** mounted to its roof, which stays in contact with the overhead line and supplies each tram's motors with electricity.

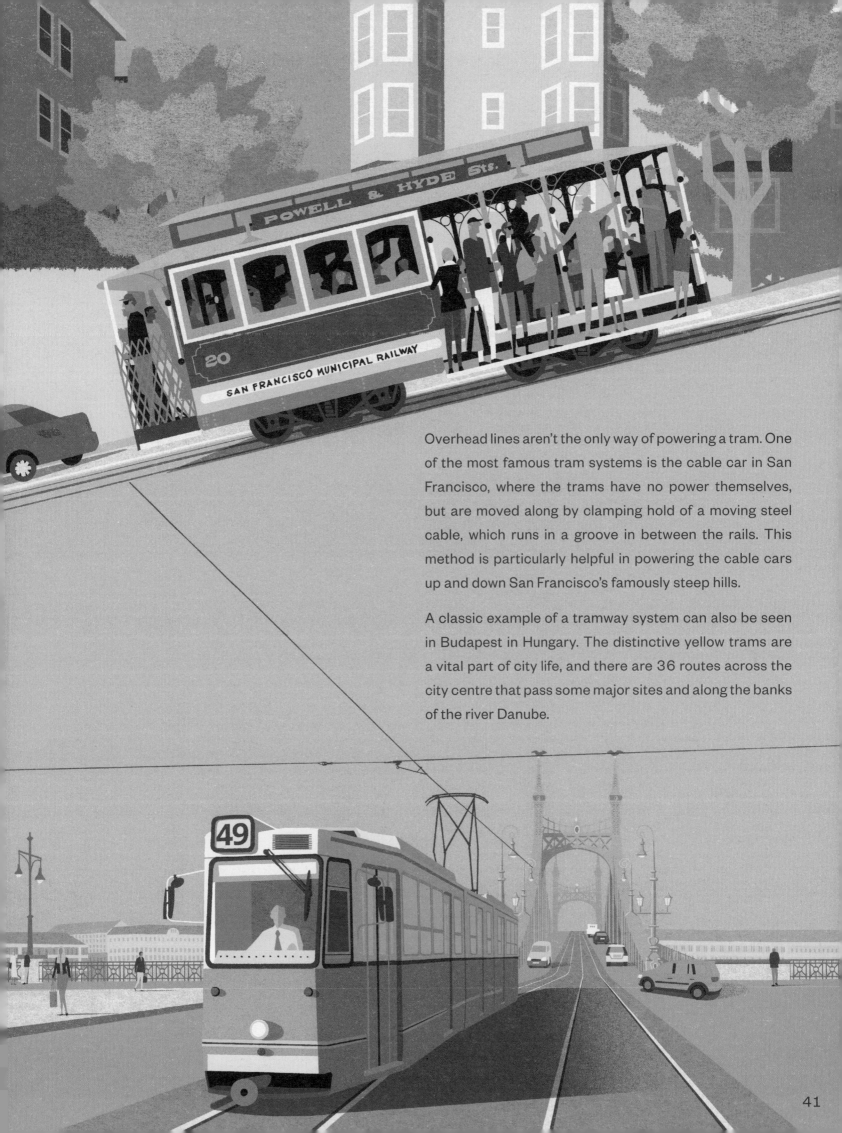

Overhead lines aren't the only way of powering a tram. One of the most famous tram systems is the cable car in San Francisco, where the trams have no power themselves, but are moved along by clamping hold of a moving steel cable, which runs in a groove in between the rails. This method is particularly helpful in powering the cable cars up and down San Francisco's famously steep hills.

A classic example of a tramway system can also be seen in Budapest in Hungary. The distinctive yellow trams are a vital part of city life, and there are 36 routes across the city centre that pass some major sites and along the banks of the river Danube.

SKY LINES

There are some railways that do not run along the ground at all, but instead are suspended above the train. These single rail systems are called 'elevated monorails'. Today they can be found around the world, most often for short urban journeys so they don't come into contact with pedestrians or other vehicles.

British engineer Henry Robinson Palmer opened one of the earliest elevated **monorails** in 1823. It was intended to help transport heavy materials using containers balanced on either side of a single overhead rail. In 1825 the first passenger elevated monorail opened, where people were pulled along in suspended carriages by a horse, paving the way for modern elevated monorails.

The Wuppertaler Schwebebahn opened in Germany in 1901 and is one of the most iconic elevated monorails today. Thought to be influenced by Palmer's early designs, it carries around 85,000 passengers every day, suspending them directly above the River Wupper for much of the route.

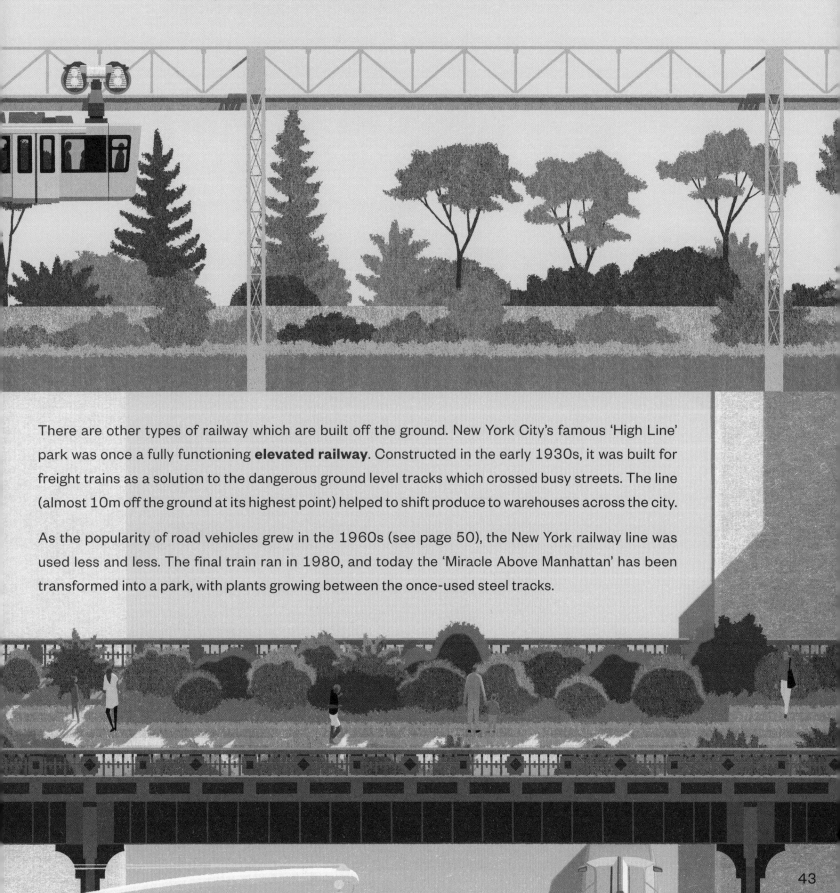

There are other types of railway which are built off the ground. New York City's famous 'High Line' park was once a fully functioning **elevated railway**. Constructed in the early 1930s, it was built for freight trains as a solution to the dangerous ground level tracks which crossed busy streets. The line (almost 10m off the ground at its highest point) helped to shift produce to warehouses across the city.

As the popularity of road vehicles grew in the 1960s (see page 50), the New York railway line was used less and less. The final train ran in 1980, and today the 'Miracle Above Manhattan' has been transformed into a park, with plants growing between the once-used steel tracks.

COMPLETE CONTROL

Safe and efficient train movements rely on the control and management of signals. Over time, control systems have developed and evolved to allow for the technical and complex industry we see today.

The Stockton and Darlington Railway ran its first train in 1825. In front of the train was a man on horseback, carrying a flag. Law stated that the public had to be warned of a train's approach, and so the first type of signalling was born.

Before long, railway lines became much busier and trains became much faster. A method was needed to let them know when to stop and start, and so time intervals were introduced. This was where a set amount of time, often around 10 minutes, was allowed between the passing of each train running at full speed. These were controlled by railway staff, who waved flags to signal to drivers.

Mechanical signals first appeared in the UK in 1841. These indicators took different forms, sometimes with discs or arms, which could be raised and lowered to signal if it was safe to proceed. These were known as 'semaphore signals'.

POSSESSION AND SIGNALLING

The interval system worked as long as the trains worked, but early trains were not reliable. When they broke down, the time intervals no longer worked. In situations where visibility was poor (such as in foggy conditions or tunnels), many accidents occurred by trains running into each other, simply because there was no way of knowing a preceding train had stopped. The solution was to divide the railway into different portions, known as block sections. In this system, only one train is allowed to enter a block at any time and is said to have 'possession' of that section of track.

Electric 'colour-light' signals were introduced in the early twentieth century and quickly became widespread. These were placed in positions along the track where they were clearly visible to the driver from some distance away. Red lights indicate 'stop' and green indicate 'proceed', similarly to road vehicle traffic lights. Today, most modern trains rely on sophisticated computer-based signalling systems displayed in the **cab**. These run automatically and can stop a train in the event of an emergency.

RAILWAYS AT WAR

By the beginning of the 20th century, railways were criss-crossing
all over the world. Cars were expensive, and air travel was in its infancy,
so many countries relied on railway networks, which were at the forefront
of efficient transportation for goods and passengers. But with the arrival
of the First World War in 1914, they were about to be pushed to their limits.

Railways were monumental in their contribution during the war. Trains were
able to provide the logistics and support required for enormous numbers of
troops on the front lines. They were at the core of transportation across Europe,
shifting millions of tonnes of military equipment, ammunition, medical supplies
and food rations every day, as well as helping to move thousands of soldiers. At
the front lines, lightly laid narrow-gauge railways transported troops and their
supplies. The tracks could easily be moved or amended as required, with small
locomotives and **handcars** snaking their way towards the trenches.

WOMEN AND CHILDREN

Some of the decisions made in wartime have had a lasting impact on the railways and the way they are run today. As men and boys were called away to fight, more women were able to gain employment in vital railway roles. In fact, the number of women working on the railways in the UK during the First World War rose from 9,000 to 50,000.

Initially some women became ticket collectors on major railways while others patrolled platforms, but as the war went on more women took on roles which had traditionally been thought of as male. This included engineering roles such as carpentry, welding and mechanical technicians, paving the way for careers that many women pursue today.

Women also played a vital role in evacuation, helping to move millions of children and vulnerable adults to safety, and away from cities which were enemy targets. In the UK, over 1.5 million people, including 800,000 children, used trains to escape to the countryside in the first three days of the Second World War with the assistance of the Women's Voluntary Service.

– RAILWAYS OF THE WORLD –
THE PRINCESS CHRISTIAN

The First World War took place between 1914 and 1918, and with it came an unprecedented number of injured soldiers. The railways took up the call to transport the wounded as quickly, comfortably and efficiently as possible, and thousands of women and men started new roles as nurses, medics and orderlies.

So-called 'ambulance trains' had already been in use in the 19th and 20th centuries, but it wasn't until the arrival of the First World War that their possibilities were fully realised. Many early ambulance trains were adapted from existing service trains, but later models were specifically built to act as moving hospitals – equipped with well-stocked pharmacies, theatres for surgery, kitchen cars and ward cars.

The *Princess Christian* (shown above) was the first purpose-built mobile ambulance train, and was jointly commissioned by the British Red Cross and Princess Christian (the daughter of Queen Victoria) in 1898 for the Boer War in South Africa. Every aspect of its design was carefully considered so as to minimise the suffering of the sick and wounded over long distances. Bunk beds were stacked three tiers high to make efficient use of the space inside, corridors were kept clear to provide walkways, and ward cars had special beds which could be raised and lowered. Beds were even fitted with shock-absorbing springs for maximum comfort.

The *Princess Christian* went on to inspire the design of several other ambulance trains, which played a vital role in saving lives throughout both world wars.

END OF THE GOLDEN AGE

If the 19th century represented the boom years for railways, then the 20th century represented their decline. In many countries, people had gained access to motor vehicles for the first time, and this freedom meant relying less on railways. In the US, non-commuter rail travel declined by 84% over the two decades following the Second World War.

In places such as Europe and Japan, much of the **infrastructure** had also been badly affected by the Second World War. With changing social and political attitudes, alongside new advances in technology, it simply didn't make sense to rebuild or maintain railways as they had been before. The decline of the railways was especially felt by rural communities, where railways had often been a valuable lifeline to the population. Nearly a quarter of Britain's railways were closed by the 1970s.

NEW OPPORTUNITIES

In the US, passenger services were widely cut back, due not only to increased road use but competition from airlines for cross-country travel. Travelling by train coast to coast would have taken three days or more, but travelling by plane dramatically reduced the journey time to just hours. Today, freight services still power across the country, providing a vital service that airlines cannot match, and doing so more efficiently and cheaply than road vehicles.

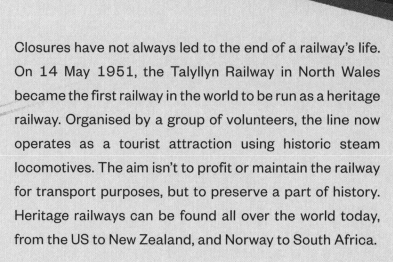

Closures have not always led to the end of a railway's life. On 14 May 1951, the Talyllyn Railway in North Wales became the first railway in the world to be run as a heritage railway. Organised by a group of volunteers, the line now operates as a tourist attraction using historic steam locomotives. The aim isn't to profit or maintain the railway for transport purposes, but to preserve a part of history. Heritage railways can be found all over the world today, from the US to New Zealand, and Norway to South Africa.

HIGH-SPEED RAIL

By 1964, the age of the jet plane was in full swing, and many people were enjoying the freedom of their own car. Trains were considered slow, obsolete and unfashionable. But the Japanese were about to open an exciting new sort of railway which was to be as revolutionary as Stephenson's *Rocket*, 140 years before. It was known as high-speed rail.

There is no fixed definition of a high-speed railway, but trains that operate above 200km/h are usually considered to be high-speed, with the fastest operating at over 300km/h. Trains which run on high-speed lines are sleek passenger services, designed to be aerodynamic to provide extra efficiency. They are also immensely powerful. High-speed trains don't require a separate locomotive, but usually have an integrated power car at either end, or powered bogies spread evenly down the length of the train. There is more to high-speed rail than just speed, though. Tracks are specially designed with gentle curves and rails that are continuously welded together to give a smooth ride.

High-speed rail became an exciting goal for many countries. In 1981, with the opening of the TGV (Train à Grande Vitesse) Sud-Est line, France became the second country to run a high-speed railway. This was the catalyst for the spread of high-speed lines across Europe, the only network to cross international borders.

Today, China has more kilometres of high-speed track than the rest of the world put together. The network not only accounts for over two-thirds of the world's high-speed railways, but also the fastest trains. The *Fuxing Hao* travels at an incredible 350km/h!

– RAILWAYS OF THE WORLD –
THE SHINKANSEN

The route between Tokyo and Osaka was the very first high-speed railway. Opened in 1964, and with a top speed of 220km/h, the iconic 'Bullet Train' became the fastest train in the world. The Shinkansen network is extraordinary for many other reasons, too. Its safety record is impeccable, with not a single passenger fatality or injury due to train accidents in its entire history. It is also so punctual that delays are measured in seconds, not minutes!

With 515km of track to construct, 67 tunnels and over 3,000 bridges to build, the project was considered too expensive by many. The eventual bill of ¥380 billion (nearly double the initial estimate of ¥200 billion) forced the president of the railway company and his chief engineer to resign before it even

opened. But the critics were soon proven wrong, and within three years over 100 million passengers had been carried across the route. This roaring success allowed the network to continue expanding despite the costs, and today Shinkansen routes stretch right around the country with more planned.

The Shinkansen network is also specially designed to deal with earthquakes (with an average of 1,500 happening in Japan every year). **Seismometers** along the route measure tremors and can automatically cut power to the lines and activate emergency brakes on the trains if required. To help monitor the track, special trains observe the condition of the rails and overhead wires. Their yellow livery and diagnostic capabilities have given them the nickname the 'Yellow Doctors'!

INTO THE FUTURE

It is estimated that by 2050, the global population will stand at almost 10 billion. With an estimated 75% of that population living in cities, railways could help to facilitate the growing demand for environmentally friendly travel. Trains have the potential to be the future of greener, cleaner transport, and there are several existing ideas which may influence the railways of the future.

As our reliance on fossil fuels decreases, diesel-powered locomotives will most likely disappear, much as steam-powered trains did a few generations ago. Electric trains emit 25–30% less carbon per mile than diesel engines, and have the potential to be powered by **renewable energy** sources, further contributing to cleaner air. One idea that is being tested is hydrogen fuel cells. These use hydrogen and oxygen as fuel, meaning that trains could one day produce their own power with an exhaust of pure water vapour.

Another exciting idea is the *Maglev train*. This stands for 'magnetic levitation', which gives some indication as to how it operates. Instead of running on conventional railway lines, the *Maglev* uses two rows of magnets set into a guide track. The first set is configured to repel the train upwards, causing it to float just above the track, while the second set pulls the train forwards. Both sets of magnets remove any friction from the track, making very high speeds possible. The fastest train ever is a *Maglev,* which achieved an astonishing 603km/h on a test track in Japan in 2015.

RESISTANCE-FREE TRAVEL

Looking even further ahead, an exciting theoretical form of train is the Vacuum Tube Train, sometimes called the *Vactrain* or *Hyperloop*. This takes some of the features of *Maglev* technology, including levitation, but goes a step further to reduce the friction – it removes the air! By placing magnetic tracks inside a sealed tube and removing the air, all resistance is completely removed. This means that extremely high speeds could be reached, certainly high hundreds, but maybe even thousands of kilometres per hour!

TRAIN TIMELINE

The history of railways and rail travel has helped bring civilisation to where it is today, from the earliest introductions of industry, through the Industrial Revolution and into the 21st century. Railways will continue their vital role in the future of transport and can be part of the answer to many of the environmental questions we are striving to solve today.

1600S
Horse-drawn coal wagons run on wooden rails.

1767
The world's first iron rails for coal wagons are used in the UK.

1825
The Stockton and Darlington Railway opens in the UK. It is the first public steam railway.

1829
Robert Stephenson's *Rocket* wins the Rainhill Trials in Liverpool, UK.

1964
Japan opens the world's first high-speed passenger railway – the Shinkansen.

1949
Canada announces abolition of steam trains, completed in 1960.

1916
The Trans-Siberian Railway is completed, spanning the width of Russia.

1913
The world's first diesel-powered train is used in Sweden.

1968
Britain's railways end the use of steam locomotives.

1981
France opens the TGV high-speed line between Lyon and Paris.

1984
The world's first commercial *Maglev* train opened at Birmingham Airport, UK.

1991
Germany opens its first high-speed rail line.

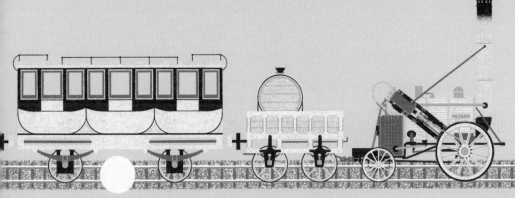

1830
The Liverpool and Manchester Railway in the UK runs its first steam passenger service.

1841
The Great Western Railway opens between London and Bristol, UK.

1856
In Mississippi, US, a railway bridge is built over the Mississippi River for the first time.

1863
The world's first underground railway (the Metropolitan Railway) opens in London, UK.

1904
The New York City Subway opens.

1890
The world's first electric underground railway opens in London, UK.

1871
The original Grand Central Terminal opens in New York, US.

1869
The first transcontinental railway is completed, spanning North America from east to west.

1994
The Channel Tunnel opens – a railway line that runs under the sea, linking England to France.

2014
Japan begins construction of *Maglev* route between Tokyo and Nagoya.

2016
The Gotthard Base Tunnel in Switzerland opens, becoming the longest railway tunnel in the world.

2020
A Virgin Hyperloop completes the first-ever trial with passengers.

RECORD BREAKERS AROUND THE WORLD

BIGGEST STEAM LOCOMOTIVE
Union Pacific Big Boy, US (1941) – 40.5m long, 548,300kg total weight

SMALLEST PUBLIC RAILWAY
Wells and Walsingham Light Railway, UK – 260mm

WIDEST GAUGE RAILWAY
Great Western Railway, UK – 2,140mm

FASTEST ELECTRIC TRAIN
TGV, France – 574.8km/h (2007)

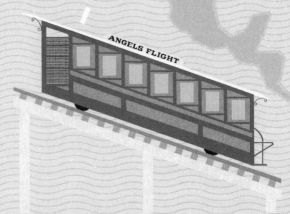

SHORTEST RAILWAY JOURNEY
Angels Flight, LA, USA – 91m

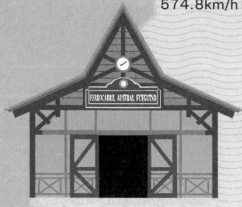

MOST SOUTHERLY STATION
Cascada de la Macarena, Argentina – opened 1909

The history of the railways is one filled with quests for speed, power and size. From the legendary *Union Pacific Big Boy*, to the mammoth *BHP Iron Ore*, here we take a look at some of the greatest railway record-breakers.

MOST NORTHERLY STATION

Karskaya, Russia – opened 2011

LONGEST TRAIN JOURNEY

Trans-Siberian Railway, Moscow to Vladivostok, Russia – 9,289km

MOST POWERFUL ELECTRIC LOCOMOTIVE

Novocherkassk 4E5K, Russia (2014) – 17,838 horsepower

DEEPEST STATION BELOW GROUND

Arsenalna, Ukraine – 105.5m below ground

HIGHEST RAILWAY STATION

Tanggula Station, China – 5.1km above sea level

LONGEST FREIGHT TRAIN

Australia BHP Iron Ore (2001) – 7.353km, 682 wagons and 8 locomotives

GLOSSARY

AIRSHIP

A type of inflatable aircraft that is made lighter than air by the use of gasses such as hydrogen or helium.

BOGIE

A set of wheels a set of attached to a frame which pivots. This helps trains to round corners more smoothly.

BOILER

The part of a locomotive where steam is produced.

CAB

Also known as the driver's compartment or footplate, this is the part of the train that houses the driver and operating crew.

CANTILEVER BRIDGE

A type of bridge built with a pair of structures known as cantilevers (a type of beam).

CARGO

Goods carried by a vehicle, such as a plane, train or ship.

CYLINDER

These house the pistons of a steam engine, with valves allowing steam to enter and exit. They are positioned alongside the wheels which they power.

ELEVATED RAILWAY

A type of urban railway where the tracks are set above street level.

FAÇADE

The outward-facing side of a building, usually the front.

FIREBOX

The chamber in which the fire of a locomotive is placed. It is usually made of copper or steel.

FRICTION

A force that causes resistance when one surface moves over another.

HANDCAR

A small, four-wheeled railway car, operated by hand.

INFRASTRUCTURE

All of the structures, buildings, and equipment which support the railway.

LIVERY

The colours, design or branding that are added to a vehicle.

LOCOMOTIVE

An engine powered by steam, diesel or electricity which pulls a train along the track.

MIGRATION

The movement of people from one location to another.

MONORAIL

A type of railway where the trains run on a single rail.

PANTOGRAPH

A device mounted to the roof of an electric train or tram, which collects electrical current from overhead wires.

PATENT

A government recognised license or recognition of specific inventions or ideas.

PISTON

A type of plunger used in steam and diesel locomotives. The piston transfers power to the wheels via high-pressured steam in a steam locomotive, or ignited diesel oil in a diesel locomotive.

RENEWABLE ENERGY

A type of energy that is sustainable. Its source will never run out. Wind and solar power are examples of renewable energy sources.

SEISMOMETER

A type of instrument that measures the direction, intensity and duration of earthquakes by detecting movement in the ground.

SUMMIT

The top, or the highest point of a hill or mountain.

TRANSCONTINENTAL

Crossing a continent.

TRANSPORTER WAGONS

A wagon or railway car used to carry other railway equipment.

TRESTLE BRIDGE

A simple bridge made of upright piers and horizontal spans.

TUNNEL BORING MACHINE

A machine which creates tunnels using a revolving cutting face, and propels itself forwards. It can be used to excavate many materials including soil and rock.

TUNNELLING SHIELD

A protective structure used during the excavation of large tunnels which provides temporary support and shields labourers from falling material.

VIADUCT

A long bridge structure, typically made up of a series of arches or steel spans.

INDEX

A

airship 15
ambulance train 48-49

B

Baikonur Cosmodrome 22-23
Batley, Claude 36
Blaenau Ffestiniog 12-13
Boer War 49
British Great Western Railway 9
Brunel, Kingdom Isambard 9
Brunel, Marc 39
Bullet Train 54
Buran 23
Burlington Bridge 30

C

California Zephyr 30-31
canal boat 6
cantilever bridge 29
Chhatrapati Shivaji Maharaj
     Terminus 36
colour-light signal 45
Compagnie Internationale des
     Wagons-Lits 18
control system 44

D

Danyang-Kunshan
     Grand Bridge 29
Darjeeling Himalayan Railway
     34-35
Deltic 15
diesel locomotive 15, 23
Diesel, Rudolf 15
double-ended locomotive 13
Double Fairlie 13
*DRG Class SVT 877 Hamburg
     Flyer* 15

E

electric locomotive 14, 61
elevated monorail 42, 43
elevated railway 43
Empire State Express 17
ETR 200 14
express train 17

F

Fairlie, Francis Robert 13
First World War 46-47, 48
Flying Hamburger 15
Flying Scotsman 17
Forth Bridge 29
freight train 20
funicular railway 33
Fuxing Hao 53

G

Gagarin, Yuri 22
gauge 9
Glenfinnan Viaduct 28
Gotthard Base Tunnel 29, 59
Grand Central 37
Greenwich Mean Time 26

H

Hedley, William 8
heritage railway 51
High Line 43
high-speed rail 52, 58
Hogwarts Express 28
Hyperloop 57, 59

I

ICE 3 14
ICE (Intercity Express) 14
Industrial Revolution 6, 58
Intercity 125 15
interval system 44, 45

J

jet plane 52

L

Lethbridge Viaduct 28
Liège-Guillemins 36
Little Wonder 13

M

Maglev 57, 58, 59
magnetic levitation 57
Maputo station 36
metropolitan 38-39, 59

milk tanker 21
mineral wagon 21
monorail 43
mountain railway 32, 34
Mount Washington
     Cog Railway 32

N

Nagelmackers, Georges 18, 19
narrow gauge 12, 13

O

Orient Express 18-19

P

Palmer, Robinson Henry 43
pantograph 40
passenger trains 16, 17
Porthmadog 12
Princess Christian 48-49
Puffing Billy 8

Q

Queen Victoria 36, 49

R

rack and pinion system 32
renewable energy 14, 56
reverse siding 35
Rocket 10, 11, 52, 58

S

Schnabel car 23
Schwyz-Stoos 33
Second World War 47, 50
seismometer 55
semaphore signal 44
Shinkansen 54-55, 58
ship 6
Soviet Union 23
spacecraft 22
space shuttle 23
Spooner, James 12
Sputnik 22
steam engine 8, 13
steam locomotive 8, 10-11, 51,
     58, 60

steel girder bridge 31
Stephenson, George 8, 10
Stephenson, Robert 10, 58
Stockton and Darlington Railway
     8, 16, 44, 58
stone hopper 21
subway 38
Swansea and Mumbles Railway
     16

T

Talyllyn Railway 51
time zone 27
toy train 34
Train à Grande Vitesse 53
tram 33, 40-41
transcontinental railway 27, 59
Trans-Siberian Railway 27, 58, 61
Travelling Post Office 24
trestle bridge 28
Trevithick, Richard 8
Tube 39
tunnel boring machine 29, 39
tunnelling shield 39

U

underground 38, 39, 59

V

Vactrain 57
Vacuum Tube Train 57
viaduct 28

W

wagon 8, 12, 16, 20, 21, 33, 58
Werner von Siemens 14
Wuppertaler Schwebebahn 43

Y

Yellow Doctors 55

Z

Zeppelin 15